THE BIG TOD! FIRST COLORING BOOK

100 PICTURES!

For questions or suggestions please contact us at admin@pghposters.com

THIS BOOK BELONGS TO:

_____

_____

Animals

Clothes

Food

Toys

At Home

Outside

Cat

Chicken

Dog

Elephant

Goldfish

Giraffe

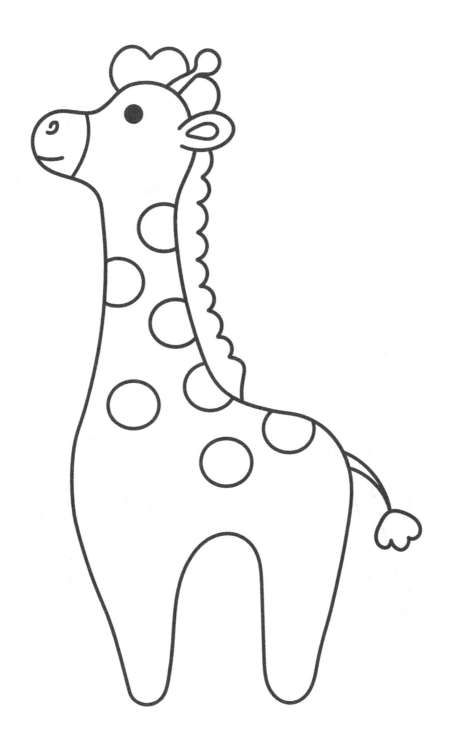

Horse

Lion

Snail

Squirrel

Rabbit

Bear

Octopus

Seahorse

Shark

Whale

Animals

Clothes

Food

Toys

At Home

Outside

Jacket

Pajamas

Dress

Pants

Shorts

Socks

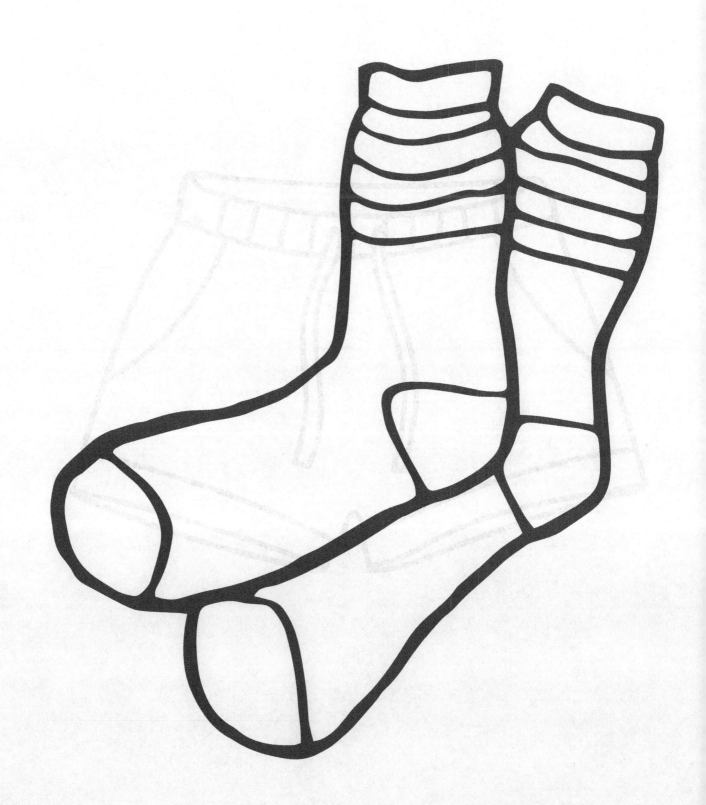

Sweater

Sneakers

Gloves

Diapers

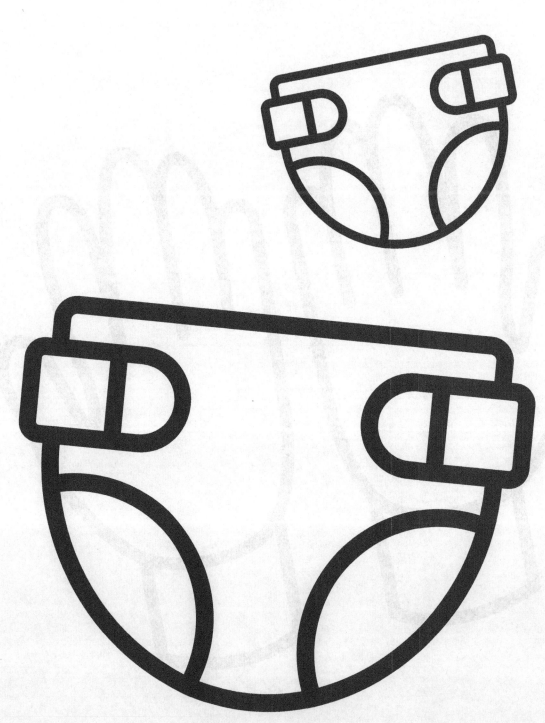

Onesie

Hat

Mittens

Flip Flops

Animals

Clothes

Food

Toys

At Home

Outside

Tomatoes

Carrots

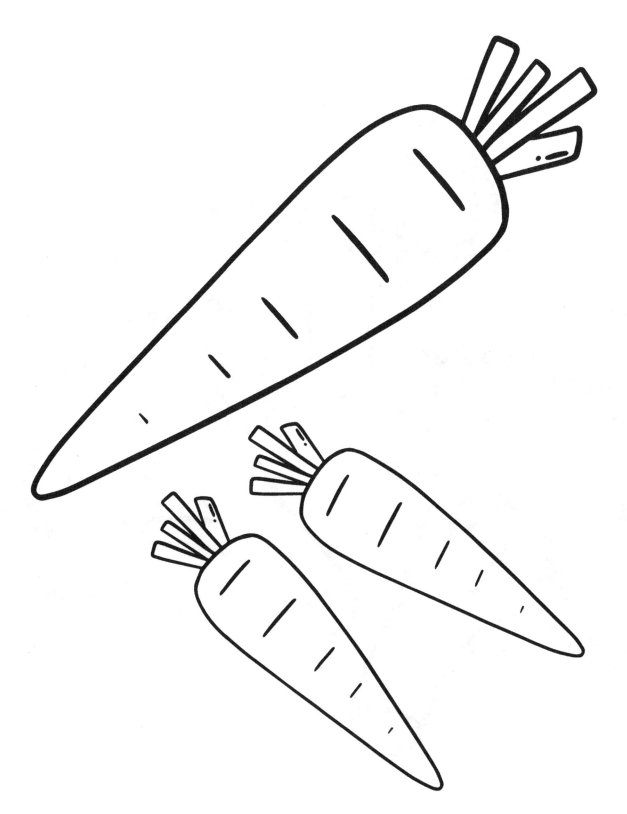

Broccoli

Pumpkin

Mushrooms

Milk

Orange Juice

Corn

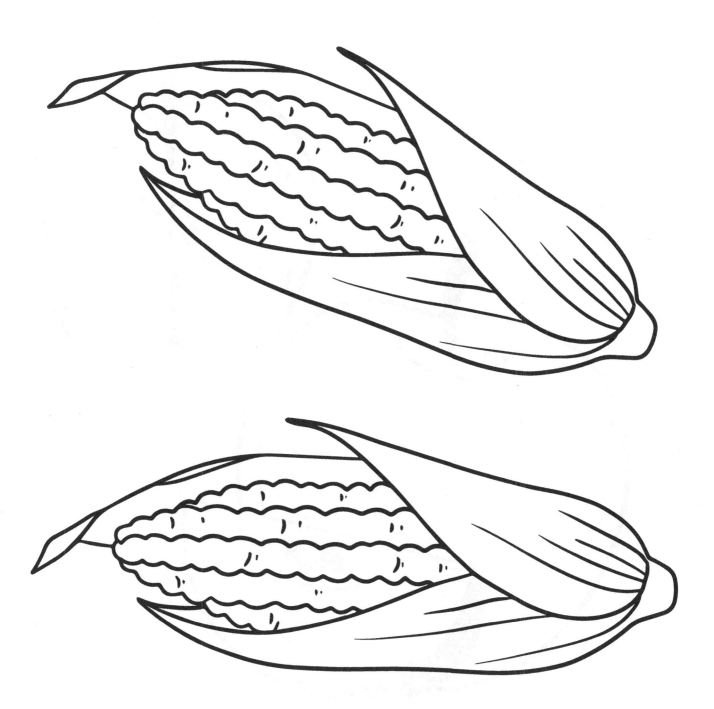

Apple

Hotdog

Sandwich

Cherries

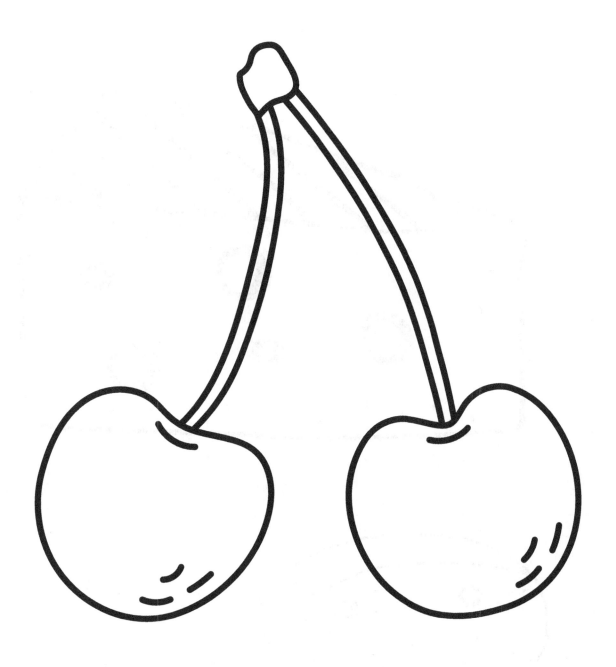

Cheese

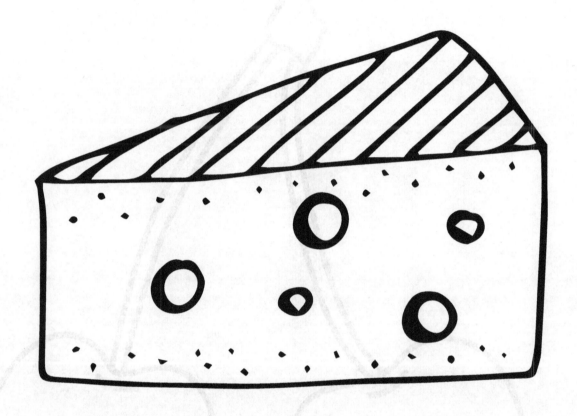

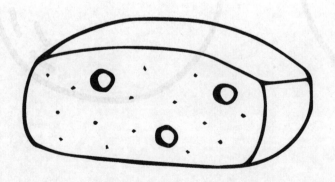

Lemon

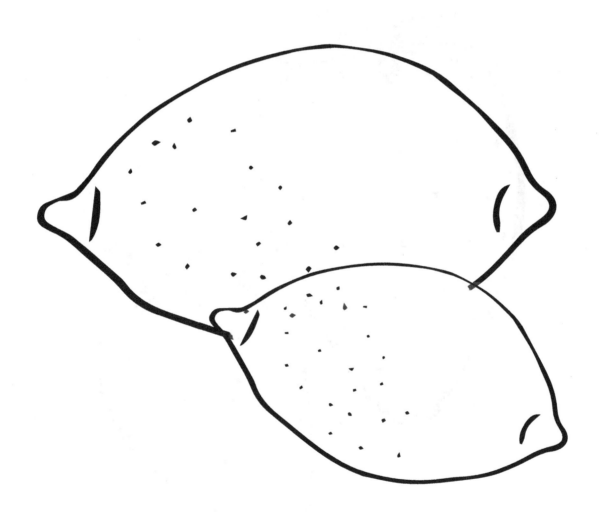

Strawberry

Pizza

Hamburger

Cupcake

Banana

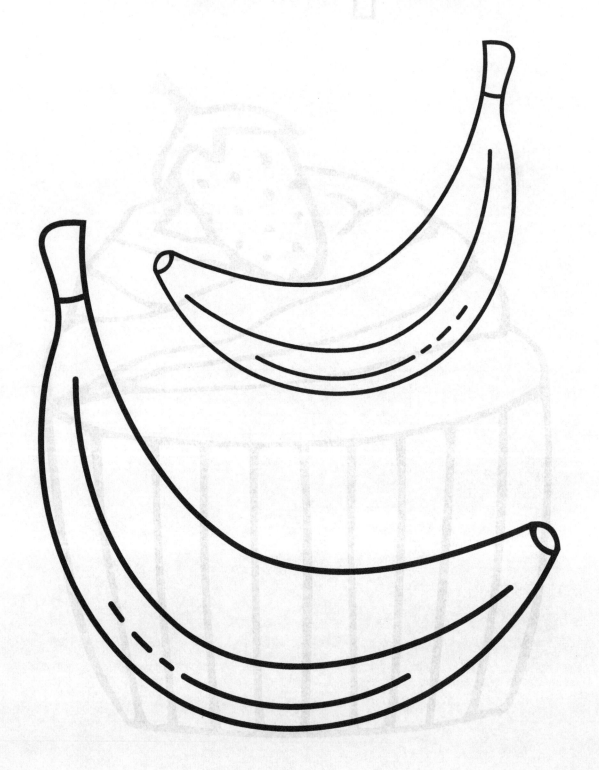

Pretzel

Popcorn

Animals

Clothes

Food

Toys

At Home

Outside

Blocks

Train

Toy Plane

Astronaut

Spaceship

Robot

Doll

Teddybear

Truck

Princess

Rubber ducky

Rocking horse

Paint

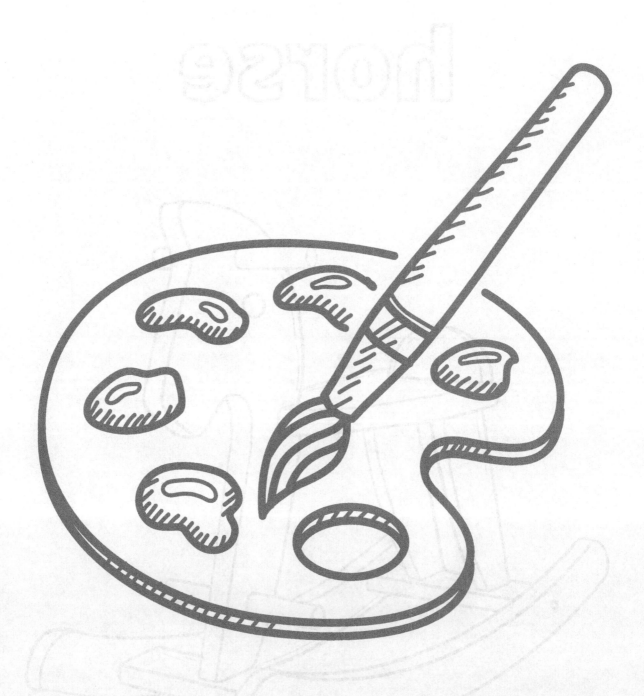

Crayons

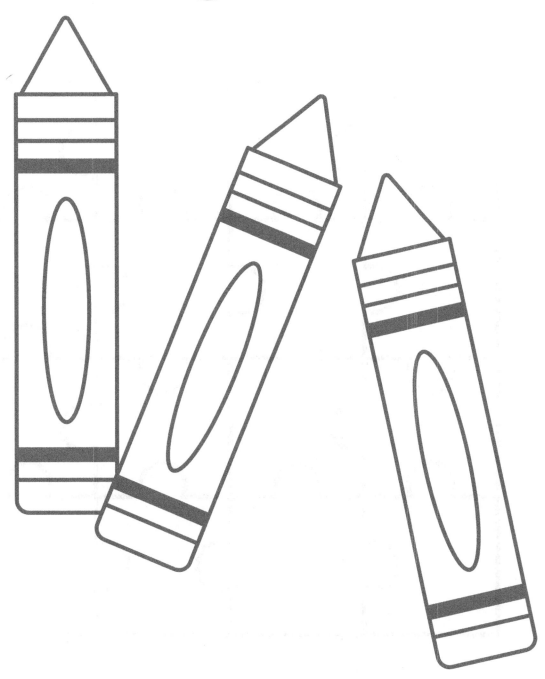

Puzzle

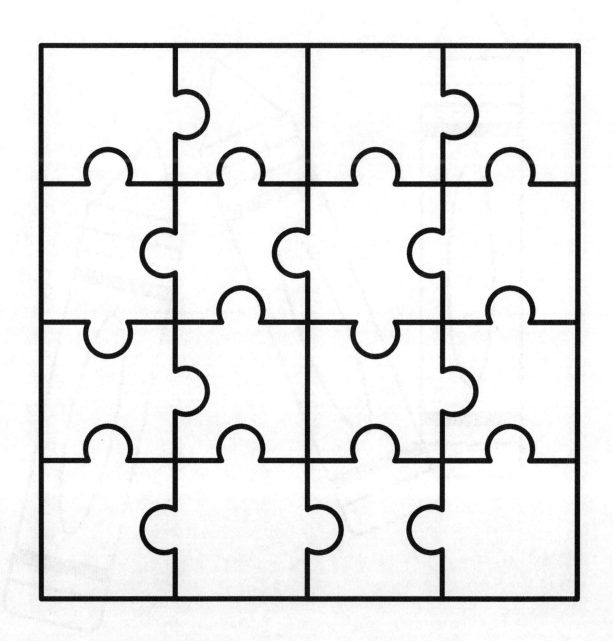

Animals

Clothes

Food

Toys

At Home

Outside

Bed

Oven

Lamp

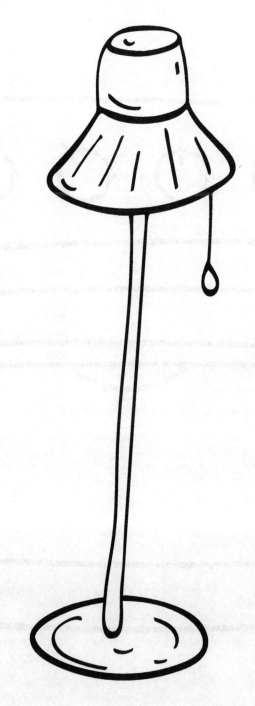

Chair

Table

Light

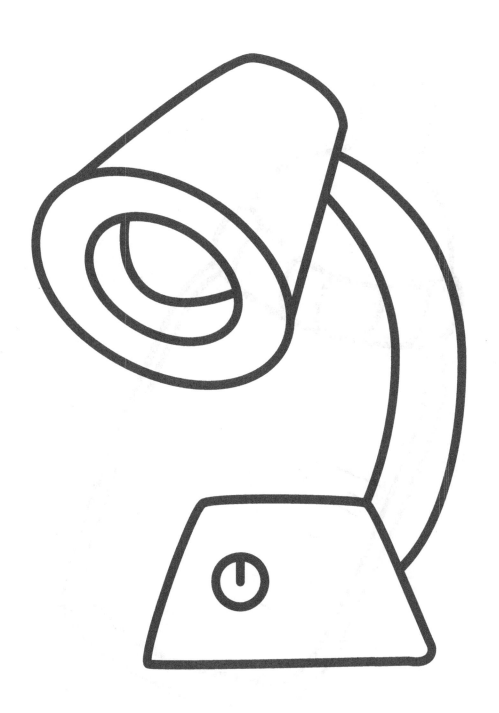

Bottle

Soap

Sink

Bathtub

Toilet

Toilet paper

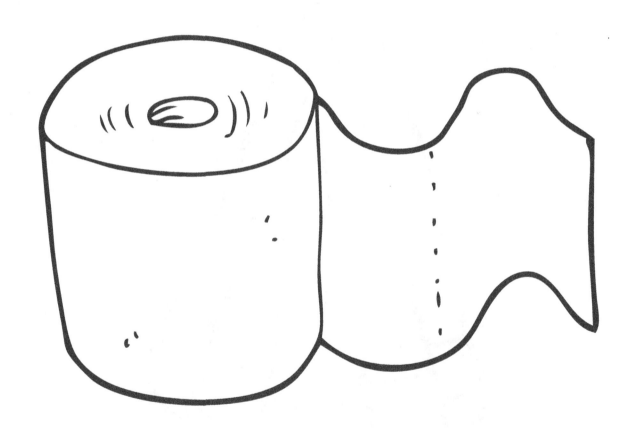

Towel

Toothbrush

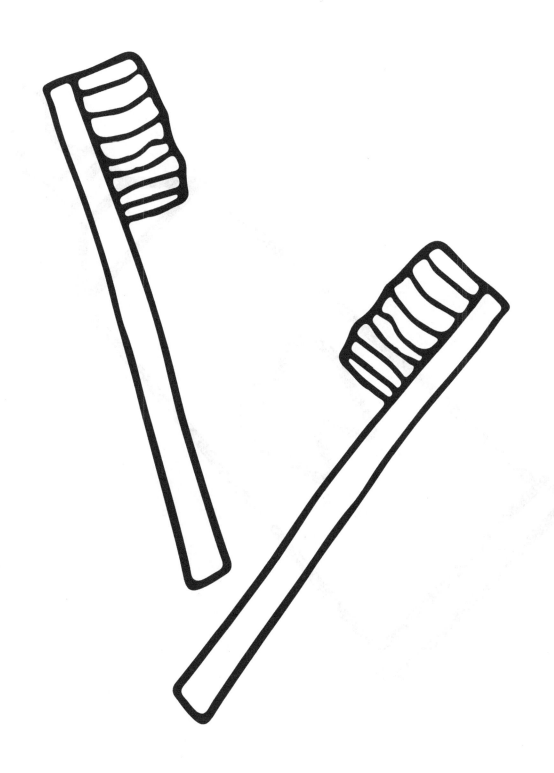

Toothpaste

Tissues

Backpack

Animals

Clothes

Food

Toys

At Home

Outside

Scooter

Bicycle

Skateboard

Motorcycle

Car

Carseat

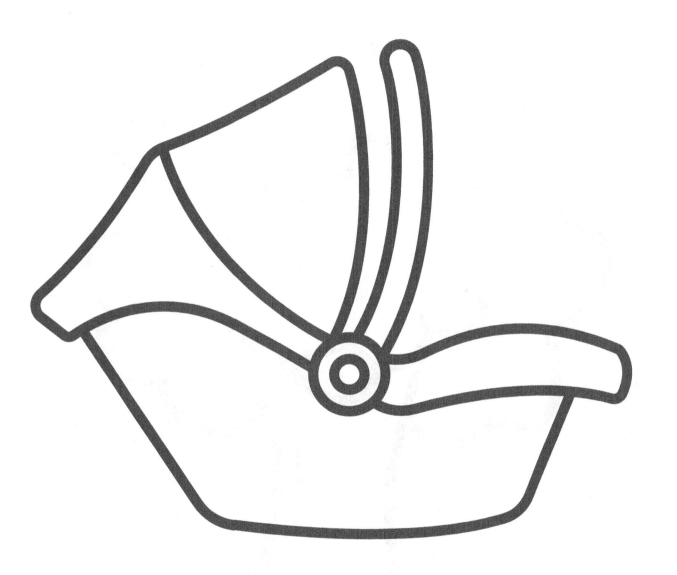

Tree

Flower

Kite

Campfire

Grass

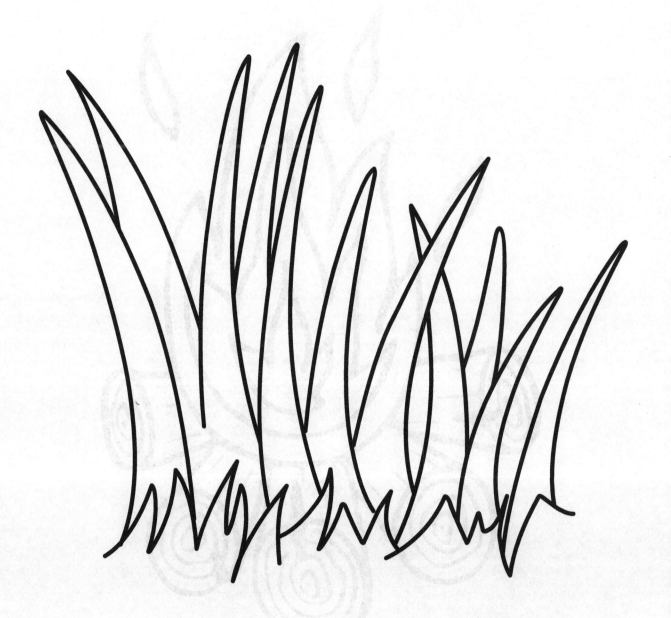

Picnic Table

Stroller

Balls

Slide

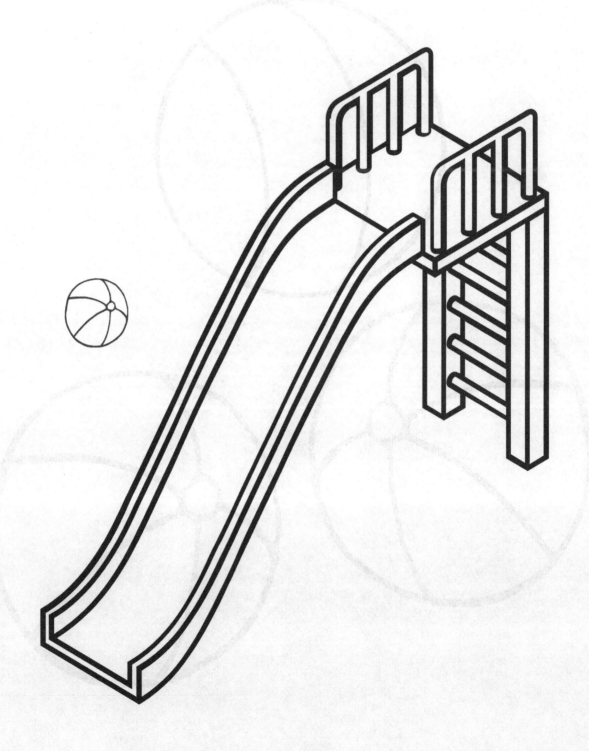

Swings

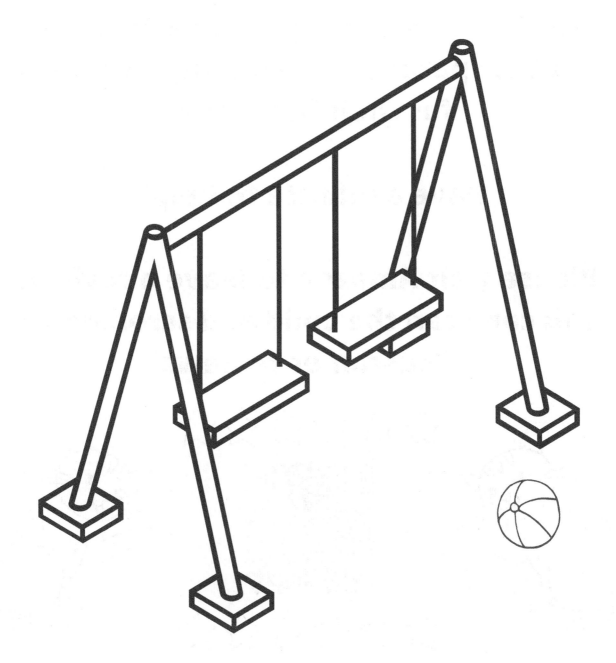

We are a family business and this is our very first book!

Having honest reviews from customers like you is extremely helpful to us and to other parents considering this book for their little one.

Have a minute to help?

Please visit Amazon to leave a review: you can scan the code and scroll down to "customer reviews".

Feel free to share pictures or video of your own little one's creations too!